THE TRAVAIL
Of The
FLAG

THE TRAVAIL
Of The
FLAG

by
Shelli Jones
Baker

New Leaf
Press

**FIRST EDITION
1989**

Painting Photo by: K.C. Photo
                     Kent Casey

Cover Art: Shelli Jones Baker

Typesetting by: A.G.A.P.E. Graphics & Printing

Library of Congress Catalog Number: 89-63069
ISBN: 0-89221-176-8

"Write the vision. Make it plain upon tables that he may run that reads it. The vision is yet for an appointed time. But at the end it shall speak and not lie. Though it tarry, wait for it as it will surely come. It will not tarry."

Habakuk 2:2

THANKS TO:

My husband Ronnie and my daughters who prayed me through this project and also Lee and Jan Morgans and Billye Brim and Elizabeth Pruitt and Gwen Shaw who all helped spread this message around the nation.

Special thanks to Shirley Bair who typed and edited the second chapter.

CONTENTS

I
dedicate
this book to
all of those who
gave their lives to
found America, "the
land of the free and the home
of the brave," and to keep
it by the guidance of the
Lord Jesus Christ
and His holy
written
Word!

Shelli Jones Baker

1

BURNING
"OLD GLORY"

Burning the flag of any nation is much more serious than a mere expression of complaint. It is and has historically been considered a universal declaration of war! For in desecrating the emblem of a nation, the assassin antagonizes and challenges its citizens to declare and determine whether or not they be indeed a worthy and honorable people at all. Lack of response is cowardice towards the mockery of their intelligence, importance, and the heritage of their children. The assailant contests their right to consume wealth, occupy valuable lands and govern endeavers that bind them as a nation.

Under the blood-stained banner of their labor and sacrifices, they are simply bound, either in weakness or strength by the constitution of their wills: mind, soul and body. America simply is the Constitution of the United States and its flag - an emblem and a mirror reflecting her people.

Awake! Awake! If we dare sleep. A battle cry has been sounded. And, America, I hear the destroyer's feet! How shall we engage him?

"The *weapons of our warfare* are not carnal, but mighty through God to the pulling down of strongholds;

"For we wrestle not against flesh and blood, but against principalities, against powers, against the rulers of the darkness of this world, against spiritual *wickedness in high places.*"

Today, this wickedness lurks in the lowly streets of the ghetto where "Old Glory" is being torched and worse yet in the high seats of the Supreme Court where its honor is being scorned. As elusive as the early markings of the Civil War, again an enemy of liberty and the Union has crept into the tidy marbled halls of Washington and established a foothold that shall be difficult to remove.

How significant are the recent Supreme Court decisions on allowing "flag burnings", Dial-a-porn, restrictions of religious symbols in public, and the executions of juveniles or the retarded and the reversals of abortion rulings? They are absolutely critical to the definition of liberty and the survival of a population accustomed to it in America!

Why? Because these rulings affecting the very core of America's moral conscience are based on the interpretation of its governing axis, the Constitution of the United States. Reactions as adverse as night and day or fire and ice have caused the document to literally go on trial! It now faces the delicate surgery of amendment and possibly (in the hands of the wrong jurors) total abolishment, punishment for a disease it does not bear and a crime it did not commit. Where stands the accuser then? He hides in the robes of the Supreme Court!

Never created to become a law-making branch of government, the child now betrays the parent into the blood thirsty mob which it has stirred up! The Supreme Court was birthed through the process of the Constitution and designed to serve the Godly conscience of our founding fathers and the new republic they hoped to guide in 1787.

Alexander Hamilton, one of the original signers, in creating three governing branches to balance the sinful and selfish nature of man with the divine providence of God,

16

stated that the Supreme Court was the least dangerous branch. In Article III of the Constitution, the writers gave the judicial branch the role of first interpreting federal statutes and *secondly* interpreting the power of the Constitution.

The court was clearly to be limited to the intent of the Constitution's framers as stated by many of the original signers in their own writings. The judges of the court were not to simply substitute the founding father's notions and ideas or to become law makers in their own right. Nor were they to rule like England's magistrates or kings for life. The latter addition to their duties was extremely adverse to the desires of the forefathers. George Washington nearly refused to be president because of the public fear of having another power-hungry king like the one they had fought in the Revolutionary War.

Chancellor James Kent, a close disciple of Alexander Hamilton, said this in the 1700's: "If judges are not bound by the intent of the founding fathers in interpreting the constitution, they are free to roam at large in the trapless fields of their own imaginations." This is exactly the ripe condition today. We are entangled in a system too large to perceive, addicted to a media saturation too convincing to disbelieve, and the result is that we have judges with almost unlimited authority ordering the most intimate affairs of our physical existence, religion and morality.

In 1987 I visited Russia on a ministers' tour and found the conditions appalling: masses of people who no longer retained the ability to govern themselves. I was surprised to learn from our government tour guide that Russia had approximately 600 million people - and not nearly all Communist as I'd grown up to believe. But only 17 million of them officially belonged to the party, and from what I could gather, most of them probably did so just to reap the benefits of a more elite lifestyle. And out of that 17 million only 5 hundred held seats in the capital affairs, and out of that number only a tiny handful of less than 10 controlled the major decision making processes that affected the entire population that I had been taught to hate.

17

I think that it is a curious thing these two governments now align themselves so closely with similar languages and systems. It becomes difficult to determine how good suddenly becomes evil - and evil, strangely sweet?

Suddenly our own constitutional law has become a fuddy-duddy fraud, a scapegoat for a system of government by the majority vote of a nine-person committee of lawyers, un-elected, and holding positions of ultimately higher influence on our lives than the president - and for life! This is the system that guided a generation to murder millions of unborn children with legal excuse. Now they tell us to burn our flag if we want to or amend the Constitution! What a wonderful choice; we declare war on ourselves as Iran and Cuba join in the folly of the flames; or we risk dissecting our governing charters beyond recogniton trying to adjust its savor to fit our modern day pallets if we speak to put the fires out. Somebody had better PRAY! We certainly need a higher power with a bird's eye view of this mess to survive the war.

As we allow our own citizens to desecrate our flag, we lose face in the eyes of the entire world. Those who have long awaited the opportunity to quench our spirit and rob our lands are licking their chops like wolves in the shadows, hardly able to believe what delights their eyes. We don't need to fear an army, a bomb, or a Hitler; if we don't repent, another Hitler will have ease to rise up in our midst. Just let some fool try to burn Russia's flag in the Kremlin Square; and he will be cremated as a courtesy of the guards for his funeral!

Who are these people burning the flag? How did its destiny become a constitutional issue of the Supreme Court?

In 1984, during the Republican National Convention in Dallas, Texas, Gregory Lee Johnson, along with other demonstrators, stole a publicly displayed American Flag and burned it screaming, "America the red, white, and blue, we spit on you." He was a member of the Revolutionary Communist Youth Brigade.

The American Civil Liberties Union came to Johnson's

defense after Dallas police arrested him for "desecration of a venerated object" and theft. Pushing the case all the way to the Supreme Court, with funding from such organizations as the Playboy Foundation, ACLU not only succeeded in declaring war on the American Flag and its residents, but won a significant series of battles as well; demolishing the sacredness of the flag, protection for pornographic publishers, illegalization of religious displays in public, etc...

In 1931 a Congressional Committee stated "The American Civil Liberties Union is closely affiliated with the Communist movement in the U.S., and fully 90 percent of its efforts are on behalf of communism..." Founder of the ACLU, Roger Baldwin, is quoted as saying, "I seek the social, ownership of property ... Communism is the goal." And Brock Chislom, director of the World Health Organization echoes this Communist and New Age theory, "To achieve World Government it is necessary to remove from the minds of men their individualism, loyalty to family tradition, national patriotism and religious dogmas..."

Clearly these people see our nationalism as the "blood clot" in the circulatory system of their efforts to undo the fabric of our flag and the government of liberty for its people. They have, like Hitler and Napolean, waged a war from within that is nearly won before the victims have realized the attack. And what have they used as their weapon? Broad misinterpretation of the Constitution!

There is truth to the fact that the First Amendment guarantees free speech, but there are just certain actions that do not benefit the rest of society's well-being. At the time that amendment was written, some of its signers were also signing bills in their state legislatures to prohibit spitting on sidewalks to prevent epidemics and blasphemy and cursings. If one man can burn the flag as an expression of free speech, then I hope another cannot speak our military secrets to an enemy and drop a bomb as his expression of equal feelings!

And there are certain things that our government owns publicly such as government buildings, equipment, and all

---

of the real estate that you and I pay taxes on. A flag is also just as equally a public piece of property no matter who sews it together. We pay no tax to the treasury for it, but we pay the dues with reverence. Forty-eight out of fifty states have laws on the books which make "flag burnings" a criminal offense which accurately portrays the governmental feeling of the past 200 years regarding the flag.

Evolution of the Stars and Stripes

1777, Sept. 14	- Design approved by Continental Congress.
1777, Nov. 1	- First time hoisted at sea, on the "Ranger," commanded by John Paul Jones, sailing from Portsmouth, NH, to Nantes, France.
1778, Jan. 28	- First time hoisted outside the United States - on Fort Nassau, Bahama Islands.
1778, Feb. 14	- First recognition by foreign power - a salute of nine guns from French fleet off Brest, France, given to the "Ranger."
1787 - 1790	- First time carried around the world - by the "Columbia," commanded by Robert Gray.
1795, May 1	- Flag of fifteen stars and fifteen stripes created by Congress.
1814, Sept. 14	- Name of "Star-Spangled Banner" given to flag by Francis Scott Key to honor defense of Fort McHenry, Baltimore, under British bombardment in War of 1812.
1818, July 4	- Flag of thirteen stripes and twenty stars becomes official. From this date on thirteen stripes remains the unchanged number; a new star added for each new state admitted to the Union on the following July 4.

1824, Mar. 17	- Name of "Old Glory" given to flag by William Driver, commander of the "Charles Doggett," at Salem, MA.
1834	- United States Army authorizes its artillery to carry the national flag as a regimental color.
1841	- Each regiment of infantry is given right to carry the Stars and Stripes.
1892	- Pledge of Allegiance to the Flag is written by James B. Upham and Francis Bellamy.
1905, Feb. 20	- Federal law prohibits registration of a trademark that "consists of or comprises the flag or coat of arms or other insignia of the United States."
1907	- United States Supreme Court upholds constitutionality of state statutes imposing penalties for desecration of national flag.
1912, Oct. 29	- President William Howard Taft's executive order establishes uniformity of design in the national flag.
1923 - 24	- National flag conferences at Washington, DC, draw up a code prescribing proper display and usage of the Stars and Stripes.
1942, Dec. 22	- Flag code becomes federal law.
1943	- United Supreme Court invalidates state laws requiring individuals to pledge allegiance to the flag.
1949, Aug. 3	- June 14 officially designated as Flag Day.
1954	- Phrase "under God" added to flag pledge.
1960, July 4	- Flag with fifty stars and thirteen stripes becomes official.

Though I feel the Constitution would stand alone if interpreted in the light of its framers on this issue of the travail of the flag, I deem it better to amend the document for its protection and pray that the changes do not exceed the need. But politics and legislation are not the answer.

I do not loathe the judges of the Supreme Court or worship the founding fathers. They are but men and women caught in the battle of the ages, that which rages between God Almighty and Lucifer, the fallen one who continuously challenges His plans to liberate Adam's race. Though many soldiers shed their blood for the cause of liberty, there has never been a drop more precious than that of God's own Son Jesus who shed His once and for all at Calvary that through its crimson flow, all men might find eternal freedom. Quoting Rev. Roy Hicks, "Earth is the only heaven a sinner will ever know and Earth is the only hell a Christian will ever have to endure!"

In studying the history of this text, I have discovered that most often the heroes are not as wonderful, and the villains are not as terrible. Legend and tradition are more deadly. But if we will dare look with eyes wide open at the truth, it will set us free from the snares that our enemy has laid for us.

Written in this text is that which I hope may provide understanding to mend wounds, unite divisions, and inspire revival of souls to Christ. God has provided cannon fodder in the annals of history and the Bible to wage our war against Satan's devisive plans of destruction. We do not need to go to blows with the tormented fellow who is burning the flag but to pray for his soul and for our leaders whom God has given power to govern. He can still turn the heart of a king!

Upon my return to New York from Russia in 1987, I heard the voice of God in my heart: "I have sent you to foreign lands before, and I will yet send you again, but now I commission you to reach America, for there is trouble in the land, and it will become to you as a foreign country, for you will traverse her highways and byways and be as a tourist or foreigner to see it as if through objective eyes." I wonderingly pondered that quietly. Then two months later The Holy Spirit poured out the most all-consuming vision upon me that has provided the fishhook for the work in that plan. There is hope.

2

PAINT THE VISION AND RUN WITH IT

"America you are too young to die!" These words of encouragement, these words of warning lingered in my ears as Colonel Bird finished his Fourth of July address. "Let us bow our heads and pray for America," he concluded. His stirring speech had not been delivered through the lips of America's firecracker-happy citizens that day, but from the heart of one who had watched her from afar with concern, through an international scope. Colonel Bird had served the United States military as the warden of Nuremburg's prison in Berlin, West Germany for over twenty years.

Not only had his words pled for America to awaken from a spiritually diseased hour of her history, but the voices of foreigners also had preambled his speech earlier in the day.

One distinguished guest from India's address had diminished to fumbling tears as he determined that America's light might soon burn out, leaving the rest of the world in utter darkness.

This is a fountain filled with blood.

Colonel Bird began to pray. I obligingly dropped my head to join him in spirit but my own thoughts obliterated his prayer.

"Die? America? Surely not our great and mighty nation! Could America ever die? Oh, God, no!" I prayed. Thoughts of her tangled domestic and foreign policy problems, the outbreak of AIDS plaques, confused moral standards, and economic upheavals flashed before me. "Surely there is some salve for her, some answer," I prayed.

God suddenly returned a startling reply. Before I could catch another breath, I found myself sovereignly consumed by His presence, dramatically involved in a vision that unfolded in 3-D all about me. It seemed as if the convention hall had vanished. Then there was a flash of something metallic. Then something wet.

"Blood!" I gasped. Spurting from smoky vapors that engulfed me was a fountain of blood. Splashing across my face and hands, a forceful flood erupted from someone's arteries. I squinted to discern whose blood.

Flashing in the wet mixture of blood and water was the outline of a gleaming metal spear. I watched its razor-sharp edge emerge from a slash of raw flesh that covered the length of a man's exposed rib-cage. Then I understood that I beheld a rare view of my precious Savior's riveted side. Animated in every detail, the vision unfolded before me as a living mural, a history of the ages painted in Jesus' blood.

Angelic voices then narrated the first scene by singing William Cowper's hymn:

"There is a fountain filled with blood,
Drawn through Emmanuel veins,
Sinners plunged beneath that flood,
Loose all their guilty stains."

My eyes followed the fountain of blood from Jesus' wound as it spread across His middle, broadened into a river, a waterfall, and then pooled into the breadth of a tumultuous ocean. The images of men baptizing converts appeared to be standing on the shores of this ocean. The shoreline became part of a continent that spread into a world map behind the crucified figure of Christ. Contrary to my theological knowledge of His death, I realized that He was not hanging on the old wooden cross but upon the nations themselves. Calvary was no longer contained to the borders of Jerusalem but occupied all the earth. For what had the weight of the cross symbolized anyway but the burden of all men's sins and the travail of all their wars spiritual and physical.

Swarming above Christ's head were stormy skies terrifyingly full of the elements of war spreading the length and breadth of all five continents. But in the midst of it all, hung His corpse seemingly as much alive as dead. Never had I thought to see a face so full of compassion and peace, yet masked with such tears of agony. His lips seemed still able to expel the last breath of a sweet blessing upon the earth. Even in death the contentment upon His face, that His work was finished, made Him appear to be a reigning king over death and the events of time and eternity.

The body was dead, but the blood continued to flow as if from an endless supply source. Its motion portrayed much life. As it lapped across the shores of the ocean it created, I saw how it washed over the turmoil of men upon those continents and healed them, silencing the voice of their sin.

Revelation jumped into my heart! Jesus' blood was shed for the healing of the nations, for their peace, restoration, and total liberty! Surely America, the greatest booster of liberty for all, could salvage a measure of that. Was this her healing salve to prevent an early death? Yes!

Even as I dared ask the question, I saw the ocean of blood take on the Atlantic's shape. Embarking upon its waters were three ships to the south, and a larger one to the north. Somehow I knew them to be those of Columbus and the Mayflower. Sailing on the water and blood from Emmanuel's side, they seemed to be carriers of the message of liberty. I watched them dock in the harbors and white sand bars of the American shoreline. The blood that carried them there flowed on past the white shores, up into the mouths of its rivers, lakes, and streams, from East to West, from sea to shining sea, until the continent of North America was striped with blood.

Scenes of the French and Indian War, American Revolutionary War, Civil War, Spanish-American War, and countless other pieces of history appeared on the map. The blood that flowed from these scenes mingled with the blood of Jesus until it formed the bold red and white stripes of courage and purity on Old Glory, our flag. Above the United States' map, bombs burst in air, and the heavenlies raged until they, too, faded into the peace of a western starry sky and became the everlasting stars of the Union as Betsy Ross had once sewn them there. I scanned the entire vision again from Christ's bleeding side, across nations in travail, to the far western shore of America where there at last was peace, an eye of calm in the storm.

"Oh, God, what have You shown me?" I hoped to know.

Again there was an answer: "The birth of a nation. Adam birthed a bride from his side, and Christ as well - not for the sake of one nation, but for all the earth. Unfolded before you is the 'Travail of the Flag.' In its fabric is not the symbolism of history alone, but waymarkers for future generations to retain their strength. By God's divine providence, this flag came to be a symbol of redemption, peace, and liberty for all nations. Ever since that plan was unfurled, jealous men and satanic forces have contested America's right to fly it as guardian over its purpose - freedom. Again and again the flag and its people have been brought to travail by the testings of spiritual and physical war." I determined to obey the Holy Spirit's prompting: "Paint the vision quickly and run with it as a herald before the eyes of the nation. It will remain in their hearts longer than a thousand sermons in their ears!"

Five days later in the heat of an Oklahoma summer, I began to paint on four fresh canvas panels totaling a dimension of 4 by 8 feet. I chose the media of acrylics, which I had never used before in one of my paintings, but chose for the haste with which they would dry and allow me to create the work. Even though God had commissioned me to paint, He had not given me a deadline for the unveiling. Yet all the while, I felt an urgency of His Spirit guiding me steadily towards some near date foreordained. At first, I painted eight hours a day; then by August, eighteen hours a day; and in late September, twenty-four hours around the clock!

In the early stages of the work, I used a brush three inches wide and continually replaced each brush with one a size smaller until the final details were painted with a brush of three hairs!

The presence of the Lord was the source of energy behind every stroke. It seemed that my studio was consumed with His presence night and day and in my weariest hours, it seemed as if angels guided my hands for support. I did not paint what I desired but was faithful only to what the Holy Spirit had shown me.

And I marveled much how He had prepared the vessel He was using. Twelve years earlier, my parents had sent me to study art at the Rhode Island School of Design but their hopes and dreams had almost been crushed when I was stricken with colitis and eye troubles early in the course of my studies. But God clearly had a plan not to be thwarted. Concerned friends took me to a prayer meeting one evening where I so encountered the presence of the Holy Spirit that I was consumed by His presence and completely healed of every symptom. The bifocals I had worn were presented to a specialist on a later date and he pronounced that my eyes had no more need of them, saying the restoration of my eyes was miraculous.

Miraculous! If the Author of the miraculous could turn one life such as mine, then surely there was hope for an entire nation!

3

AMERICA! GOD SHED HIS GRACE ON THEE

Completed in less than three months, fifteen hundred hours of work waited to be unveiled before the eyes of the nation on October 11, 1987. Two of my dear friends, Elizabeth Pruitt and Billye Brim, had intercepted the painting before its completion and decided to plan the ceremony for me with the assistance of my pastors, Lee and Jan Morgans, at A Glorious Church Fellowship in Collinsville, Oklahoma. My mother and a friend had flown in to accept the honor of drawing back the veil. Rev. Kenneth and Gloria Copeland previewed the painting and prayed a first benediction upon the task of showing it to the nation, prophesying that it would be used to turn the heart of Congress one day.

All of the power and might of Almighty God's prophetic voice seemed to be focused on America through the point of my paint brush. I was as curious as anyone as to what the many images that lay behind that veil would mean as we began to pull it back to give us the interpretations.

Muffled sighs, gasps, and weeping touched God's heart as I began to sing the "Star-Spangled Banner" and mother pulled back the drape.

Oh say can you see?

Oh, say can you see
Through the dawn's early light
What so proudly we hailed
At the twilight's last gleaming
Whose broad stripes and bright stars
Through the perilous fight
O'er the ramparts we watched
Were so gallantly streaming
And the rockets' red glare
The bombs bursting in air
Gave proof through the night
That our flag was still there.

Oh, say does that Star-Spangled Banner yet wave
O'er the land of the free and the home of the brave?

On the shore dimly seen
Through the midst of the deep
Where the foes haughty host
In dead silence reposes.
What is that which the breeze
O'er the towering steep,
As it fitfully blows,
Half conceals, half discloses.
Now it catches the gleam
Of the morning's first beam.
In full glory reflected
Now it shines on the stream.

Tis the Star-Spangled Banner Oh long may it wave
O'er the land of the free And the home of the brave.

And where is that band
Who so vauntingly swore
That the havoc of war
And the battle's confusion
A home and a country
Should leave us no more?

Their blood has washed out
Their foul footsteps'pollution.
No refuge could save
The hireling and slave
From the terror of flight
Or the gloom of the grave!

And the Star-Spangled Banner in triumph doth wave
O'er the land of the free and the home of the brave.

Oh! Thus be it ever
When free men shall stand
Between their loved homes
And the foe's desolation;
Blessed with victory and peace,
May our Heaven's rescued land
Praise the Power that hath made
And preserved us a nation.
Then conquer we must,
For our cause it is just -
And this be our motto:
"In God is our trust!"

And the Star-Spangled Banner in triumph shall wave
O'er the land of the free and the home of the brave!

As I finished singing these words penned by Francis
Scott Key during the War of 1812, I wondered why America
did not sing the last verse on the few occasions when the anthem is still sung. Key had called America "Heaven's
rescued land!" America had first learned to sing this majestic
crest swelling anthem with pride in God rather than self.

After unveiling the painting, I dared not move because
the glory of God hung around us so thick that we could see
what seemed like a mist in the church. All eyes were fixed on
the painting. I turned to view it and was awestruck by the
anointing upon it. I felt that I had carried it as a baby, but
now it had been delivered to stand on its own. I realized that

it did not belong to me but to the nation. I saw how I had not authored its design or its strokes God had! Now it ministered as much to me as to anyone else.

The "Travail of the Flag" seemed to be alive with a heavenly beauty as it stood on the platform in its new guilded frame. Andres Sorens, a naturalized citizen from Latvia, had donated the frame, having fashioned it himself without any prior woodworking experience. Having lost his freedom once in life at the age of eight during the clash of the co-invasion of Nazi Germany and Russia, he cherished the liberty portrayed in the painting. He donated the frame to give the painting its crowning glory from the hands of all those who had lost their freedom with the hope and prayer that America would never lose hers!

How precious freedom is to those who have none, dear enough to shed blood for it.

While curious eyes surveyed the painting for the first time, I began to sing another patriotic hymn, "America the Beautiful," by Samuel A.Ward,

> Oh,beautiful for spacious skies
> For amber waves of grain,
> For purple mountains' majesty
> Above the fruited plains.
> America, America,
> God shed His grace on thee;
> And crowned thy good with brotherhood
> From sea to shining sea.

My hand traced the blood which flowed from Jesus' side, westward through the Atlantic, across the red strips of America and the battlefields of her brotherhood. "God shed His grace on thee."

> Oh, beautiful for pilgrim's feet
> Whose stern impassion'd stressed
> A thoroughfare for freedom beat
> Across the wilderness.

America, America,
God mend thy every flaw
Confirm thy soul with self control
Thy liberty in law.

Oh, beautiful, for hero's feet
Proved in liberating strife;
Who more than self their country loved
And mercy more than life.
America, America,
May God thy gold refine
Till all success be nobleness
And every gain divine.

Oh, beautiful for patriot's dream
That sees beyond the years;
Whose alabaster cities gleam
Undimmed by human tears.
America, America,
God shed His grace on thee
And crowned thy good with brotherhood
From sea to shining sea!

Who were the patriots? What kind of people were they? Like us today or different in courage and belief? What was their dream that saw beyond the years? Why had they shed their human tears in liberating strife; loving their country and mercy more than their own lives and comfortable gracious living?

4

CHOSEN FOR REVIVAL

Many are called; few are chosen. To simply obey the calling of God is to be chosen. It is very simple.

"Are you your brother's keeper?" God asked Cain after he slew Abel. God said that Cain was to have been his brother's keeper.

I am my brother's keeper. I painted a painting to help my fellow American. Those patriots who shed their blood were my keepers. They have made me to be my brother's keeper over lands where I have yet to go. My passport can take me there, but it was bought with their blood to keep me free. It says I am in blood covenant with those who died for the liberty to worship Jesus Christ and believe in Him. A nation who does not respect innocent blood will soon lose her liberty.

Look at Germany and Russia. Before their dictators brought them to their political suicides, they both were murdering babies and Jews or Christians. And, Oh God, now look at us who have slaughtered over 2.1 million babies in abortion clinics since 1973.

My passport says I am ready to shed my blood if need be and that I uphold the Constitution. But America has become a nation of covenant breakers. Newspaper headlines and articles, T.V. shows and gossip columns continuously report divorces, broken military truces, corruption of financial institutions, and most recently "flag burnings"!

From ancient times governing powers have displayed their intents to serve the covenants of their gods on coins, military objects and symbols. America still displays the founding fathers' faith on coins that boast "In God We Trust". The inscriptions on the marble halls of Congress and the Supreme Court remind the statesmen and lawmakers of God's divine providence to guide their feet in battle and their decisions of which He desires to be a part. But who entreats easily the vocal expression of a patriotic citizen these days?

In March of 1987 I was invited to minister at a church in Philadelphia. It was very near a district that was famous for the burning of an entire city block due to the extraction of a dangerous cult group known as the "MOVE" earlier in the 1980's. During one of the evening services the pastor turned to me on the platform and said, "Sister, do whatever the Holy Ghost tells you to do." Because the hour was late, I determined to take that as a hint and close the service. Laying on the podium was my recorder flute which I had used in ministry earlier in the service. When I turned back to the congregation, it caught my eye, and suddenly the inspiration came to me that I should pick it up and play "The Battle Hymn of the Republic" like a pied piper, leading the people out the door!

My face must have betrayed the shock of my flesh as it reacted to that leading of the Holy Ghost, for while I was hesitating the pastor turned to me again and said, "Sister, obey God!" We did.

Filing out the door, some fifty saints, the pastor, and my co-worker followed me singing "Mine eyes have seen the glory of the coming of the Lord..." No sooner had we filed past the parking lot on a route around the block than we came upon several teenage boys running out of an alley as

38

fast as they could, carrying bags of tools and possibly weapons or loot over their shoulders. Never was any hoodlum so shocked as these to be apprehended by the glory of God! Realizing that they had been stopped abruptly in the middle of some crime, I did not halt our march but continued on, looking back over my shoulder to see what God might accomplish. Panic paralyzed them as they searched for another escape route while some 50 saints marched by them singing "Glory Glory Hallelujah!" At last they bolted away into the night. I often wonder what effect that had upon them afterwards.

Upon completing our little "mission" we were greeted by a police car at the church parking lot. An officer informed us that at 11:00, the precise moment of departure from the church, a dispatcher had received a call concerning the theft of a car from those very premises. It turned out to be the pastor's mother-in-law's car which revealed signs of the steering column having been stripped. Piecing the events of the night together, we realized that the Holy Ghost's bizzare prompting to march had been the very thing that had surprised the boys, forcing them to hide in the alley, never dreaming that we would then apprehend them red-handed while we were singing a hymn! Instant obedience to the Holy Ghost saved the car and maybe even lives, if the confrontation with the police had ever materialized!

Facing natural circumstances, it would be ludicrous to do such a thing in a boarded up ghetto in the midnight hours. But the anointing of God can cause those who know Him to boldly recover territory and souls! When these saints saw these sinners in their path, it excited them. The glory gave them boldness. When you are fishing, it can be boring until you get a nibble. But when you hook one and then another, and another, it gets exciting! As soon as you get a nibble on your hook, your adrenalin begins to flow and you want to try again. It's just getting people to go fishing the first time that's difficult.

After this stirring adventure the pastor awarded me a van and the commission to take some members to Constitution Square. We were to lay our hands on the bell as a point of contact to pray for religious freedom. But when we entered the monument, we were unobliged and intimidated by a foreboding silence like that which prevails in a morgue.

I have encountered that kind of thing before in Russia, prison land! On a train traveling between Leningrad and Moscow that same year, I had been very aware of how guarded our freedoms were to be. However at the strong urging of a Russian orthodox priest and some 70 tourists, I was persuaded to sing the same hymn. Pulling into the Moscow station, we were some 70 voices strong, shaking the rail car with stomping feet and the glory of God! One little Russian orthodox lady was so touched that she stated, "This is a day in history; someone should write it down. Here we are the oldest known church of Russia joined in one voice with you evangelicals proclaiming the coming of the Lord in a train filled with glory in an atheistic forbidden Communist land!"

There was faith in that Russian train to be bold to proclaim freedom because the people having little of such pled to God for it, but in America we are a slumbering Samson who take our liberties and duties for granted. It's time to wake up!

Though the public proclamation of faith came easily in Russia, surprisingly, it was much more difficult in Philadelphia where no one seemingly would understand the necessity of such a gesture. My small band of crusaders and I prayed timidly at best. Then a lady dressed in revolutionary war costume for the benefit of tourism passed by and heard us praying. Surmising that we were from a church and on a mission, she kindly encouraged us to enjoy our visit to the bell and do what we had come to do. Receiving permission, we began again to sing "The Battle Hymn of the Republic".

About that time a tour of school children came in. For the first time in their lives they were seeing the Liberty Bell. Our song seemed to mesmerize them and create an imaginative atmosphere where they could more easily comprehend the purpose of the bell. What a wonderful memory to walk away with: the memory of a bell tried for religious freedom and the words from the hymn "Mine eyes have seen the glory of the coming of the Lord..." Their teachers were at first silent; then they began to mouth the words with us:

> Mine eyes have seen the glory
> Of the coming of the Lord;
> He is trampling out the vintage
> Where the grapes of wrath are stored;
> He hath loosed the fateful lightning
> Of His terrible swift sword;
> His truth is marching on.
>
> Glory! glory, hallelujah!
> Glory! glory, hallelujah!
> His truth is marching on.
>
> I have seen Him in the watch fires
> Of a hundred circling camps;
> We are building Him an altar
> In the evening dews and damps;
> I can see His righteous sentence
> By our dim but flaring lamps; (Prayer meetings!)
> His day is marching on.
>
> Glory! glory, hallelujah!
> Glory! glory, hallelujah!
> His truth is marching on.
>
> He has sounded forth the trumpet
> That shall never sound retreat;
> He is sifting out the hearts of men
> Before His judgment seat.
> O be swift, my soul, to answer Him!
> Be jubilant, my feet!
> Our God is marching on!
>
> Glory! glory, hallelujah!
> Glory! glory, hallelujah!
> His truth is marching on.

In the beauty of the lilies
Christ was born across the sea,
With a glory in His bosom
That transfigures you and me:
As He died to make men holy,
Let us die to make men free;
While God is marching on.

Glory! glory, hallelujah!
Glory! glory, hallelujah!
His truth is marching on.

(Julia Ward Howe)

The park guard was touched too. She gave us a special speech telling how the bell had not always been referred to as the Liberty Bell during its active years of tolling for freedom.

This symbol of American freedom received the name "Liberty Bell" from the description of a Biblical inscription on its rim; Leviticus 25:10:

> "Proclaim liberty through out all the
> land to all the captives thereof."

Molded in iron by patriots, forgotten by their sons, this bold declaration of purpose was not brought to light until the retirement of the bell after 100 years of service. A crack in the bell had been noticed in 1829 but had not been attended to until the damage was unrepairable.

The Holy Spirit spoke to my heart and said, "Yes, when you fail to use your liberty, you *lose* your liberty." He said, "There is a serious crack in America's liberty today, a crack in her Christianity. The bell that she was supposed to be ringing in the spirit has almost gone numb. But you tell them all across America that the damage is not yet irreparable. There is still time."

5

THEY SAILED
FOR LIBERTY

I believe that the erosions in our Christian liberties can actually be repaired. Let us proclaim those liberties, holding up the blood stained banner, "Ol' Glory," that our forefathers died to keep. As the freest people on earth, we should be able to use our liberty to do more for the cause of freedom and spreading the Gospel than any other people. I even suggest that our judgment shall have extra weight added to the scales, tipping against us if we do not. As the freest people on earth, what will we do to preserve the redeeming message of Christ's blood? For *only* "where the Spirit of the Lord is shall there be liberty." (II Cor 3:17) Without a mighty revival, we shall surely fail for lack of courage.

Fear did not prevent me from ministering in the foreboding atmospheres of Russia and Philadelphia because the anointing of the Holy Spirit was on me. This same anointing of boldness and liberty has also rested upon others who knew their God and obeyed His callings to arise and do exploits. Though ordinary and few in number, God made them strong in the face of great impossibilities and by their sacrificial lives laid out His plans and purposes for America.

In the early 15th century, the winds of the Holy Spirit began to stir the heart of a young Italian Catholic named Christopher Columbus whose name in Latin literally means "light bearer" or "Christ-bearer." A vision of God revealed to him the virgin western hemisphere and her native inhabitants, still concealed in the Creator's hand awaiting a discoverer who would draw back the curtain of time and unveil a glorious purpose: the birthing of a "Christian" nation. Certainly Columbus did not comprehend this - nor did Europe, emerging from the Dark Ages guided only by the light of human torches burning the flesh of Pentecostals and Jews.

While satanic vices worked to quench the liberty of the Gospel, God moved to open a window of refuge through Columbus, providing the only modern day haven for religious freedom. Consumed by this vision, Columbus penned these lines in a diary entitled "Prophesies."

> "The fact that the gospel should
> be preached in so many lands in
> such a short time this convinces
> me."

Thus he set out in life to obtain the goal, visiting the kings of Europe's wealthiest nations, hoping to obtain favor for the financing of his journeys. Though well educated for the task and cunning enough to offer future conquests of land and resources to the greedy palate of a king, Columbus did not succeed alone. Not until Columbus resigned the matter to God on the doorstep of a Fransiscan monastery did the first glimmer of hope appear.

Padre Juan Perez de Marchenan at the Church of Santa Maria de Rabida in Spain, led Columbus in a prayer pledging a vow to God to perform his heavenly commission no matter what the cost.

Immediately favor and financing became available

I simply went where the mind of the Holy Spirit blew me.

through Queen Isabella of Spain. Fitting into the pattern of Biblical confrontations between God's will and earthly sovereigns (like Nebuchadnezzar and Cyrus), Queen Isabella graciously supported God's ultimate plan to provide religious freedom to the very groups of people imprisoned by the horrible inquisition of her own court's design.

Written in another passage from Columbus's diary is the account of his departure from Palos Spain on Friday, August the 3rd, 1492:

> "Queen Isabella said 'Are you ready, Christopher Columbus?'
>
> He replied, 'God is with me this hour and I could not be more ready.'
>
> Queen Isabella: 'If our Lord gives you His blessings, then who am I to deny mine? God's speed ahead, Columbus!'"

God has always had His men on the threshold of discovery and technology. Jews like Albert Einstein derived their theories of science from Biblical passages, and born-again Christians pilot our space shuttles and invent intricate guidance systems for the moon launches based on visions in prayer coupled with education. The excellence of God appears to be the brilliance of Columbus's ingenious navigations as well stated further in his diary:

> "It was the Lord who put it into my mind. I could feel His hand upon me there was no question that the inspiration was from the Holy Spirit because He comforted me with rays of marvelous illumination through the Scriptures and the execution of the journey. *I simply went where the winds of the Holy Spirit blew me.*"

Pure intentions and enthusiastic words fill the first pages of Columbus's diary but his God-given plan was soon brought to travail. Three sailing vessels - the Pina, Nina, and

Santa Maria - had not only been provided by the Queen but also subsidized by a wealthy Palos family, the Pinzons. Their intention was not to sail for souls but for gold.

This kind of greed has been the spoiling of many revivals and plans of God. Calling humanity to embark on unchartered waters, and to leap beyond the unknown by faith in order to bring us to the shores of a better place physically and spiritually, God provides gold to finance the move. Unfortunately some charlatans and hecklers follow in the wake, proclaiming that the plans will fail or perverting the prosperity attached to them, having no anointing to maintain a steady course because of impure motives.

During Columbus's voyage, his men became increasingly distraught as they observed him traversing more furlongs of the unknown Atlantic than any predecessor. Such fear gripped their hearts and the hearts of the Pinzon brothers, who feared loss of their investments in the voyage, that a rebellious scheme of mutiny arose against Columbus. However, he challenged them to allow the period of 3 more days for the sighting of land at which time he would return to Spain if defeated.

During those days like Jonah he retreated to the belly of the sea-going vessel and there recounted the marvelous vision and workings of God that had brought him thus far. While he prayed, God was at work, causing the ship to traverse more furlongs of sea in a fast wind than those which she previously had traveled from Spain. A paralyzing fear of God fell upon the crew, preventing the further organizing of their mutinies. And on the third day floating vegetation from nearby land was sighted, and announced by the ship's cannons!

On Friday, October the 12th, 1492, a rapturous joy filled the hearts of the "Christ-bearers" as Columbus beheld the natives of his boyhood vision curiously hailing his vessel from the tropical island of the Caribbean Sea. With much gratitude he knelt reverently on its shore and named the island "San Salvador", "San" meaning holy and "Salvador" meaning savior.

Soon the news of the kind, gift-bearing white man spread excitedly via native tongues from one island to the next until Columbus reached the San Blas Indians of Panama. Paddling through the shallow harbor with gold rings dangling from their noses, they came expectantly to greet him. But the long-awaited sight of gold struck the Pinzon brothers with "gold fever". The meeting soon turned from a great missionary possibility into a bloody massacre as they began to torture the natives in hopes of being led to rich stashes of gold treasure.

Returning to Spain with a cargo of both Indians and gold, Columbus's success was instant - and so was his downfall. "For mine own sake ... I will not give my glory unto another." (Isaiah 48:11) Whether it was the same "gold fever" or pride which changed his heart's course, Columbus never fulfilled his original mission completely. For instead of being known as the "Christbearer", local American Indians spread his fame from the Florida Keys to Nova Scotia as "the thieving devil". Thus the plan of God to evangelize the American Indian has not yet been fulfilled. Instead of being known as prosperous Christian nations, Central and South America are poverty-stricken and under the atheistic governments of communism, for the most part. 497 years later missionaries are only now beginning to reverse the curse.

Such was the spiritual condition of Northern America 128 years later in 1620 when another ship with spiritual purpose chartered a course towards its northeastern coastline. However, this time the message of Christ's redeeming blood would not halt at the harbor as in Columbus's day but be spread throughout all the tributaries and crevices of the continent by a better prepared people, the Mayflower's pilgrims.

Educated by the benefit of the Gutenberg Press and King James Bibles of the 16th and 17th centuries in the language of the common man, these Christians seized their liberties and fled religious persecution in England, pursuing a God-given vision to colonize a "free" Christian world.

Lest anyone convince you that God was not in the

founding roots of our nation you need only direct them to the words of important documents penned by our fore-fathers - such as the Mayflower Compact, whereby one can see how the Holy Spirit became the master weaver of the fabric of this nation, thereby setting a pattern for any nation that will embrace the same Gospel of Jesus.

The very first line of the Mayflower Compact on November 11, 1620 reads:

"In the name of God, Amen."

Their intent is clearly expressed and agreed upon unanimously as indicated by their signatures in the following documentation:

THE MAYFLOWER COMPACT
November 11, 1620

"In The Name of God, Amen, We, whose names are underwritten, the Loyal Subjects of our dread Sovereign Lord King *James,* by the Grace of God, of *Great Britain, France,* and *Ireland,* King, *Defender of the Faith,* &c. *Having under-taken for the Glory of God, and Advancement of the Christian Faith,* and the Honour of our King and Country, a Voyage to plant the first colony in the northern Parts of Virginia; Do by these Presents, solemnly and mutually in the Presence of God and one another, covenant and combine ourselves together into a civil Body Politick, for our better Ordering and Preservation, and Fur-therance of the Ends aforesaid; And by Virtue hereof do enact, constitute, and frame, such just and equal Laws, Ordinances, Acts, Constitutions, and Offices, from time to time, as shall be thought most meet and convenient for the general Good of the Colony; unto which we promise all due Sub-mission and Obedience. In WITNESS whereof we have hereunto subscribed our names at *Cape Cod* the eleventh of *November,* in the Reign of our Sovereign Lord King *James* of *England, France,* and *Ireland,* the eighteenth and of *Scotland,* the fifty-fourth. *Anno Domini,* 1620.

Mr. John Carver	Mr. Stephen Hopkins
Mr. William Bradford	Digery Priest
Mr. Edward Winslow	Thomas Williams
Mr. William Brewster	Gilbert Winslow
Isaac Allerton	Edmund Margesson
Miles Standish	Peter Brown
John Alden	Richard Bitteridge
John Turner	George Soule
Francis Eaton	Edward Tilly
James Chilton	John Tilly
John Craxton	Francis Cooke
John Billington	Thomas Rogers
Joses Fletcher	Thomas Tinker
John Goodman	John Ridgate
Mr. Samuel Fuller	Edward Fuller
Mr. Christopher	Richard Clark
Martin	Richard Gardiner
Mr. William Mullins	Mr. John Allerton
Mr. William White	Thomas English
Mr. Richard Warren	Edward Doten
John Howland	Edward Liester

This was the very first document ordering government in this land, born through continuous praying and fasting. God was showing forth His guidance as can clearly be seen in my painting where Christ's right hand is laid upon England. But as in earlier times of unfolding His plans, God's enemies would bring this venture to travail also.

While sailing 63 days towards Virginia, the Mayflower encountered a vicious storm which blew it many miles off course. During the storm, one of the hired crewmen began to taunt the Puritan pilgrims for their audacious faith in God, for believing that they could possibly survive the perils of the Atlantic and furthermore the hostile environment of America's wilderness beyond it. In the midst of his mockery he was suddenly taken ill with scurvy, and he perished. Other astounded hecklers ceased in their tauntings of the landlubbers and soon joined them in the singing of a hymn led by the devout Governor William Brewster. During the subsequent time of worship the storm is said to have ceased and the hull of the ship, to have instantly risen in the hazardous waves some 3 feet, raising the draft and setting it out of danger. Shortly thereafter, on November 9, 1620, they landed in Cape Cod Harbor.

The pilgrims had gone through a lot. They had been forced to leave half of their expedition in Plymouth, England because another consigned vessel - "the Speedwell" - was not seaworthy. And they witnessed the deaths of more than forty of their passengers. Even so, they persevered and continued to trust in God. Eventually they built their colony in Massachusettes Bay. Having survived a harrowing winter of famine and death, they reluctantly waved good-bye to the Mayflower on her return voyage to England in March, 1621. As earthly securities departed, God's heavenly connections began to provide.

> "From whom the whole body fitly joined together and compacted by that which every joint supplieth, according to the effectual working in the measure of every part, maketh increase of the body unto the edifying of itself in love..."
>
> (Ephesians 4:16)

Within a week of the Mayflower's departure, an unusual Indian fellow suddenly appeared at the edge of the pilgrim settlement. Earlier encounters with hostile Nausite savages prompted the settlers to react by raising their muskets. To their utter astonishment, the Indian replied, "Welcome, Englishmen!" and went on to greet them in the name of Jesus in English. His name was Samoset, and he was from the Wampanog tribe, having learned English from previous explorers fishing off the coast. He was graciously entertained by the pilgrims with great wonderment as to what relationship God might construct for His purposes. A few days later Samoset returned with Squanto, an Indian chief from the Patoxan tribe.

Squanto's whole life had been seemingly arranged by the hand of God to prepare a guide and protection for the pilgrims. In 1614 Squanto and 20 braves had been kidnaped by an explorer named Hunt and sold in Spain as slaves. A monastery purchased and converted him to Jesus with the intent of returning him to his own people as a missionary of Catholicism. But he escaped to Protestant England in 1619 where he learned English and returned to America seven months prior to the pilgrims' arrival.

Bitter disappointment awaited him in America, for during his absence, an epidemic of disease had wiped out his entire tribe, leaving their plowed fields and dwellings in a useless condition. Gravely distraught, Squanto had sought shelter in the village of a neighboring chief, Massasoit, where he befriended Samoset as well.

The arrival of the Puritan pilgrims suddenly gave Squanto a much needed purpose for living as he soon became their interpreter and survival teacher. Likewise, it was a fortunate thing that these Englishmen had made this valuable contact and that they had just happened to have settled upon the very plot of land abandoned by Squanto's deceased tribe. Not only were the leveled cornfields an advantage but also the fact that the plague of their deceased caused other superstitious savages to avoid the area, thereby providing the only haven of safety for hundreds of miles around!

Led through many perils by a God-given desire for liberty, these pilgrims were clearly guided by His hand to a prepared place and time when the dream could be fulfilled. Though not the first to pursue this goal, they were the first to press through tribulation, willing to lay down their lives to obtain the goal, a "free" Christian nation. "Precious in the sight of the Lord is the death of one of His saints." (Psalm 116:15)

Birth from the womb comes not but by the first delivering signs of blood and water, and likewise liberty and Christianity could not have come but by that which sprang forth through the life giving-flow of Christ's side and those who travail for the Gospel's sake.

6

A NEW BREED

The pilgrims had come with no other desire but to serve God, but within one hundred years they had opened the doors for others to follow them with different desires of self-gain. But that's the mercy of God working. He opens a way for the rain to fall on the just and the unjust alike. The following documents of American History truly proclaim our forefathers strong belief in Jesus Christ and teaching it.

MASSACHUSETTS SCHOOL LAW OF 1642
April 14, 1642
(E.P. Cubberley, ed. *Readings in the History of Education*, p. 298-9)

"This is the earliest known law on education in the American colonies. Similar laws were adopted, somewhat later, by Connecticut, New Haven, and Plymouth. See also, the law of 1647, Doc. No. 20. See bibliography in M.W. Jernegan, *The American Colonies*, p. 164.

"This Cort, taking into consideration the great neglect of many parents & masters in training up their children in learning & labor, & other implyments which may be proffitable to the common wealth, do hereupon order and decree, that in euery towne ye chosen men appointed for managing the prudentiall affajres of the same shall henceforth stand charged with the care of the redresse of this evill, so as they shalbee sufficiently punished by fines for the neglect thereof, upon presentment of the grand jury, or other information or complaint in any Court within this jurisdiction; and for this end they, or the greater number of them, shall have power to take account from time to time of all parents and masters, and of their children, concerning their calling and implyment of their children, especially of their ability to read & understand the principles of religion & the capitall lawes of this country."

THE NEW ENGLAND CONFEDERATION
May 19, 1643
(F.N. Thorpe, *Federal and State Constitutions,*
Vol. I, p. 77 ff.)

"Whereas we all came into these parts of America with one and the same end and aim, namely, to advance the Kingdom of our Lord Jesus Christ and to enjoy the liberties of the Gospel in purity with peace..."

Within these one hundred years, cities had sprung up, mills, harbors, and factories. Great theological institutions to train preachers such as Harvard and Princeton came into being, but also pubs and houses of prostitution. The streets of Boston were unsafe due to murder and theft. There were pubs full of men whose dreams had been shattered by the oppressive powers of England. And in that time it looked like America's evangelical pursuit was lost and the dream of democracy, a failing experiment.

Drinking away their sorrows, brawling, thieving, raping, 18th century Americans were a fitter lot for hell than heaven. Yawning parishioners, who sparsely dotted the empty pews of Sunday meeting houses could, for the most part, no longer realize the meaning of the religious freedom for which their grandfathers had risked their lives.

It seemed that the power of Christ's crimson flow had ceased to lap against American shores. The body of Christ in America was beginning to stink like a dried-up rotten corpse! One might have thought that should the winds of revival blow, it would have already have been too late. But blow they did! And loud enough to sound like Jesus' shout of resurrection power at the tomb of Lazarus!

God chose an unlikely humble servant to breathe through, as His billows stoked the dying embers of Puritan Christianity into a flaming bonfire of *revival*! A new breed of preachers came on the scene of the **Great Awakening** as it became known.

God raised up Jonathan Edwards, a man without charismatic appeal, seemingly not the proper candidate for such an earthshaking task. But one night the faithful pastor of North Hampton, Massachusettes felt inspired to pen a sermon entitled, "Sinners in the hand of an Angry God", using as his text "Their foot shall slide in due time." (Deuteronomy 32:35)

He simply read the sermon on a hot and boring Sunday afternoon but excitement followed because God kindled the spark sovereignly, because He was ready to move across America! God moved through ordinary people as He is ready to move now! He began to burn the land of America with the fires of the Holy Ghost. The absence of true Holy Ghost fire is without doubt the sleeping potion of American churches today.

People were so stirred by Edwards's sermon that they clung to the pillars of the church crying out for salvation. They emptied out bars and closed whole towns of such to repent and be saved. Edwards preached that true Christians evidenced a change in their lives after conversion that could be seen. I believe our American churches in the present 20th century are full of parishioners who have not hungered after God with serious concern for their souls. Theirs is not a humble life of self-denial, prayers, and fasts which should allow the Holy Spirit to seal their hearts with a scar of circumcision. Of course that denotes they are in covenant with a God whose privilege it is to consume their sacrifice of total service.

Serving God as a circuit preacher, another saint arose to the forefront of the 18th century revival, George Whitefield. He was perhaps the most famous of his colleagues, even known by many as "The Great Awakener".

Befriended by John Wesley of England, Whitefield became a member of the "Holy Club" and learned there to travail in prayer for his own sin-sick soul. Inspired by a revelation of justification by faith in Christ's redeeming blood, he began preaching in the coal mines. Soon his converts, outnumbering the prestigious churches of the era, began to suffer great persecution for their efforts from jealous religious leaders. Spreading his wings in America, Whitefield continued to bear down on the religious communities in open-air meetings - like an eagle after its prey.

A marked trait of Whitefield's revival was that denominational barriers among religious foundations seemed to fall flat. One notable example is of a meeting he preached among mixed congregations of more than a thousand who heard this sermon:

Whitefield shouting into the heavens, "Father Abraham, have you any Baptists up there?" - silence - "I said, 'Father Abraham, have you any Episcopalians up there?' " - silence -. Continuing the pattern he proceeded to name every major denomination known to the crowd until at last he shrugged his shoulders and changed his position as if to preach on without the heavenly reply. Suddenly, cupping his hand to his ear he excitedly announced to the curious audience, "Father Abraham says, 'No my son, we only have Christians up here!' "

Here is an eye witness account of one such meeting which took place in a day when men and women could not advertise by phone, television, or postal services.

Mr. Whitefield Preaches in Middletown

On October 23, 1740, George Whitefield came to preach in Middletown, Connecticut. The following eyewitness account by Nathan Cole, a local farmer and carpenter, reveals the enthusiasm with which colonial Americans took advantage of the opportunity to hear George Whitefield preach:

Now it pleased God to send Mr. Whitefield into this land; and my hearing of his preaching at Philadelphia, like one of the old apostles, and many thousands flocking to hear him preach the Gospel, and great numbers were converted to Christ, I felt the Spirit of God drawing me by conviction; I longed to see and hear him and wished he would come this way. I heard he was come to New York and the Jerseys and great multitudes flocking after him under great concern for their souls which brought on my concern more and more, hoping soon to see him; but next I heard he was at Long Island, then at Boston, and next at Northampton.

Then on a sudden, in the morning about 8 or 9 of the clock there came a messenger and said Mr. Whitefield preached at Hartford and Wethersfield yesterday and is to preach at Middletown this morning at ten of the clock. I was in my field at work. I dropped my tool that I had in my hand and ran home to my wife, telling her to make ready quickly to go and hear Mr. Whitefield preach at Middletown, then ran to my pasture for my horse with all my might, fearing that I should be too late. Having my horse, I with my wife soon mounted the horse and went forward as fast as I thought the horse could bear; and when my horse got much out of breath, I would get down and put my wife on the saddle and bid her ride as fast as she could and not stop or slack for me except I bade her, and so I would run until I was much out of breath and then mount my horse again, and so I did several times to favour my horse. We improved every moment to get along as if we were fleeing for our lives, all the while fearing we should be too late to hear the sermon, for we had twelve miles to ride double in little more than an hour and we went round by the upper housen parish.

And when we came within about half a mile or a mile of the road that comes down from Hartford, Wethersfield, and Stepney to Middletown, on high land I saw before me a cloud of fog arising. I first thought it came from the great river, but as I came nearer the road I heard a noise of horses' feet coming down the road, and this cloud was a cloud of dust made by the horses' feet. It arose some rods into the air over the tops of hills and trees; and when I came within about 20 rods of the road, I could see men and horses slipping along in the cloud like shadows, and as I drew nearer it seemed like a steady stream of horses and their riders, scarcely a horse more than his length behind another, all of a lather and foam with sweat, their breath rolling out of their nostrils every jump. Every horse seemed to go with all his might to carry his rider to hear news from heaven for the saving of souls. It made me tremble to see the sight, how the world was in a struggle. I found a vacancy between two horses to slip in mine and my wife said "Law, our clothes will be all spoiled, see how they look," for they were so covered with dust that they looked almost all of a colour, coats, hats, shirts, and horse. We went down in the stream but heard no man speak a word all the way for 3 miles but every one pressing forward in great haste; and when we got to Middletown old meeting house, there was a great multitude, it was said to be 3 or 4,000 of people, assembled together.

We dismounted and shook off our dust, and the ministers were then coming to the meeting house. I turned and looked towards the Great River and saw the ferry boats running swift backward and forward bringing over loads of people, and the oars rowed nimble and quick. Everything, men, horses, and boats seemed to be struggling for life. The land and banks over the river looked black with people and horses; all along the 12 miles I saw no man at work in his field, but all seemed to be gone.

When I saw Mr. Whitefield come upon the scaffold, he looked almost angelical; a young, slim, slender youth, before some thousands of people with a bold undaunted countenance. And my hearing how God was with him everywhere as he came along, it solemnized my mind and put me into a trembling fear before he began to preach; for he looked as if he were clothed with authority from the Great God, and a sweet solemn solemnity sat upon his brow, and my hearing him preach gave me a heart wound. By God's blessing, my old foundation was broken up, and I saw that my righteousness would not save me.[1]

[1]The foregoing is a passage from the *Spiritual Travels* of Nathan Cole. It was reprinted in *The William and Mary Quarterly*, 3rd Series, vii (1950), pp. 590, 591, and subsequently in *George Whitefield's Journals* (Banner of Truth Trust: Carlisle, Pennsylvania, 1960), pp. 561, 562.

Whitefield managed to unite the colonies in spirit and purpose.

I know an elderly man in Churchville, Maryland, Mr. Scarborough, who was the organist in a Presbyterian church that grew from one of Whitefield's revivals held on his great-grandfather's property nearby. He said that men seated in chestnut trees for a bird's eye view of the sermon had been knocked to the ground by the glory of God during the meetings.

George Whitefield's blazing career included thousands of open-air tent meetings, at least seven trips across the Atlantic and untold hundreds of thousands of conversions. Finally his health broke after preaching one last sermon with two congested lungs to several thousand people in Exlter, Massachusettes. The following morning on September the 30th, 1770, he passed to heaven.

Preaching more than 8,000 sermons in a few short years, he managed to bring about an unprecedented unity of Christian spirit in the heart and mind of the thirteen colonies. Some historians attribute these massive conversions to Jesus to that one factor of moral strength which enabled the meager minute man militia of 1776 to overpower England's world-conquering armies in the Revolutionary War. Even President Calvin Coolidge was once quoted as saying, "America was born in a revival of religion and back of it were John Wesley and George Whitefield."

Other ministers such as missionary David Brainard helped to accelerate the awakening even in the long-awaited camps of the Indians.

A new breed of preachers had arrived on the scene just in time to awaken Americans to the impending perils of war, both spiritually and physically. As the Church revived in great victories, Satan's fury began to attack her. England, startled by the alarming move among colonists to ignore the constrictions of the official Anglican Church, began to raid the meetings and arrest revivalists. And King George III became increasingly intolerant of their claims to economic and governmental liberties.

A foreboding cloud of destruction, principalities and powers of Satan, began to press toward the colony. But they found the populace freshly bathed in the baptismal waters of salvation and the doorposts of their hearts cleansed with Christ's redeeming blood!

In Exodus 4:12 one sees the promise of God to honor this condition:

> "And the blood shall be to you a token upon the houses where you are: and when I see the blood I will pass over you and the plague shall not be upon you to destroy you when I smite the land of Egypt."

Their Egypt was England, and its system had to be purged so that God's plan for liberty might spring forth.

As King George III pressed increasing regulations and taxes against them, the colonist began to cry out, "No King but King Jesus!" The blood of the Revolution was shed for the sake of Jesus' Gospel and the liberties and prosperities that are produced by it. Our veterans may not understand why they lost their blood to this dear extent, but it was precious to God and the strength of our liberty today.

In the 20th century how do we stand in the destroyer's path? Is the blood of Jesus, the Lamb, applied to the doorposts of our hearts as it should be? Or will our sin-ridden bodies, too sluggish to dodge the destroyer's blows, slump upon the doorsills of the land? As former generations flying the banner have endured travail, who are we to suppose it shall not come to us to do so as well?

In 1776 men who believed they could dare to trust God for the wisdom to govern themselves signed the Declaration of Independence. I wove this into the land and fabric of the flag with my brush and painted below it a Quaker woman praying, for prayer was the only ingredient that would cause the declaration to work.

For every victory seen in the battlefields of America there were the unseen victories fought beforehand by prayer warriors on their knees behind the scenes. I know of one ac-

Washington was known to be a devout man of prayer.

count of Whitefield's converts praying all night in a corn-flower field near Churchville, Maryland while General Washington and his armies happened to be crossing the Delaware River. They had been interceding as the outcome of the war weighed in a delicate balance until news of Washington's certain victory reached them.

General George Washington himself was known to be a devout man of prayer. Though unschooled in some disciplines of Christian character, he nevertheless led a life accustomed to prayer. As a young colonel in the earlier French and Indian War, Washington records how an Indian chief testified to him that in trying many times to shoot him, it was as if great beings surrounding Washington prevented the arrows from their course. In one battle charge that he later led against the British, he did not lose a single man while the opponent's casualties numbered near a thousand. This is similar to Old Testament Bible stories of battles which Israel won through the miraculous interventions of angels. A newspaper article has been discovered from a reprint of officer Anthony Sherman's eyewitness account in the National Tribute, Vol. 4, No. 12, December 1880.

WASHINGTON'S VISION

George Washington was born on February 22, 1732. Few military figures in history ever faced misery and deprivation as did Washington and his forces at Valley Forge in the winter of 1777-1778. But three years later British General Charles Cornwallis surrendered to Washington at Yorktown to end the American Revolutionary War.

The following is a well-documented accounting of a vision General Washington had at Valley Forge.

More than a century ago a Mr. Wesley Bradshaw published an article in which he quoted Anthony Sherman, who was an officer with General George Washington at Valley Forge.

Bradshaw's original article was reprinted in the *National Tribune,* Vol. 4, No. 12, for December, 1880. He told of the last time he saw Anthony Sherman, and these are Bradshaw's words:

The last time I ever saw Anthony Sherman was on the fourth of July, 1859, in Independence Square. He was then ninety-nine years old, and becoming very feeble. But though so old, his dimming eyes rekindled as he gazed upon Independence Hall, which he came to visit once more.

"Let us go into the hall," he said. "I want to tell you of an incident of Washington's life - one which no one alive knows of except myself; and, if you life you will, before long, see it verified.

"From the opening of the Revolution we experienced all phases of fortune, now good and now ill, one time victorious and another conquered. The darkest period we had, I think, was when Washington after several reverses, retreated to Valley Forge, where he resolved to pass the winter of 1777. Ah! I have often seen the tears coursing down our dear commander's care-worn cheeks, as he would be conversing with a confidential officer about the condition of his poor soldiers. You have doubtless heard the story of Washington's going into the thicket to pray. Well, it was not only true, but he used often to pray in secret for aid and comfort from God, the interposition of whose Divine Providence brought us safely through the darkest days of tribulation.

"One day, I remember it well, the chilly winds whistled through the leafless trees, though the sky was cloudless and the sun shone brightly, he remained in his quarters nearly all the afternoon alone. When he came out I noticed that his face was a shade paler than usual, and there seemed to be something on his mind of more than ordinary importance. Returning just after dusk, he dispatched an orderly to the quarters of the officer I mention who was presently in attendance. After a preliminary conversation of about half an hour, Washington, gazing upon his companion with that strange look of dignity which only he alone could command, said to the latter:

" 'I do not know whether it is owing to the anxiety of my mind, or what, but this afternoon as I was sitting at this table engaged in preparing a dispatch, something seemed to disturb me. Looking up, I beheld standing opposite me a singularly beautiful female. So astonished was I, for I had given strict orders not to be disturbed, that it was some moments before I found language to inquire into the cause of her presence. A second, a third, and even a fourth time did I repeat my question, but received no answer from my mysterious visitor except a slight raising of her eyes. By this time I felt strange sensations spreading through me. I would have risen but the riveted gaze of the being before me rendered volition impossible. I asssayed once more to address her, but my tongue had become useless. Even thought itself had become paralyzed. A new influence, mysterious, potent, irresistible, took possession of me. All I could do was to gaze steadily vacantly at my unknown visitant. Gradually the surrounding atmosphere seemed as though becoming filled with sensations, and luminous. Everything about me seemed to rarefy, the mysterious visitor herself becoming more airy and yet more distinct to my sight than ever before. I now began to feel as one dying, or rather to experience the sensations which I have sometimes imagined accompany dissolution. I did not think, I did not reason, I did not move; all were alike impossible. I was only conscious of gazing fixedly, vacantly at my companion.

The First Peril

" 'Presently I heard a voice saying, "Son of the Republic, look and learn," while at the same time my visitor extended her arm eastwardly. I now beheld a heavy white vapor at some distance rising fold upon fold. This gradually dissipated, and I looked upon a strange scene. Before me lay spread out in one vast plain all the countries of the world - Europe, Asia, Africa, and America. I saw rolling and tossing between Europe and America the billows of the Atlantic, and between Asia and America lay the Pacific. "Son of the Republic," said the same mysterious voice as before, "Look and learn." At that moment I beheld a dark, shadowy being, like an angel, standing, or rather floating in mid-air, between Europe and America. Dipping water out of the ocean in the hollow of each hand, he sprinkled some upon America with his right hand, while with his left hand he cast some on Europe. Immediately a cloud raised from these countries, and joined in mid-ocean. For a while it remained stationary, and then moved slowly westward, until it enveloped America in its murky folds. Sharp flashes of lightning gleamed through it at intervals, and I heard the smothered groans and cries of the American people.
" 'A second time the angel dipped water from the ocean, and sprinkled it out as before. The dark cloud was then drawn back to the ocean, in whose heaving billows it sank from view.

The Growth of America

" 'A third time I heard the mysterious voice saying, "Son of the Republic, look and learn." I cast my eyes upon America and beheld villages and towns and cities springing up one after another until the whole land from the Atlantic to the Pacific was dotted with them. Again, I heard the mysterious voice say, "Son of the Republic, the end of the century cometh, look and learn."

The Second Peril

" 'At this the dark shadowy angel turned his face southward, and from Africa I saw an ill-omened spectre approach our land. It flitted slowly over every town and city of the latter. The inhabitants presently set themselves in battle array against each other. As I continued looking I saw a bright angel, on whose brow rested a crown of light, on which was traced the word "Union," bearing the American flag which he placed between the divided nation, and said, "Remember ye are brethren." Instantly, the inhabitants, casting away their weapons became friends once more, and united around the National Standard.

The Third Peril

" 'And again I heard the mysterious voice saying, "Son of the Republic, look and learn." At this the dark, shadowly angel placed a trumpet to his mouth, and blew three distinct blasts; he sprinkled it upon Europe, Asia, and Africa. Then my eyes beheld a fearful scene: from each of these countries arose thick, black clouds that were soon joined into one. And throughout this mass there gleamed a dark red light by which I saw hordes of armed men, who, moving by with the cloud, marched by land and sailed by sea to America, which country was enveloped in the volume of cloud. And I dimly saw these vast armies devastate the whole country and burn the villages, towns and cities that I beheld springing up. As my ears listened to the thundering of the cannon, clashing of swords, and the shouts and cries of millions in mortal combat, I heard again the mysterious voice saying "Son of the Republic, look and learn." When the voice had ceased, the dark shadowy angel placed his trumpet once more to his mouth, and blew a long and fearful blast.

" 'Instantly a light as of a thousand suns shone down from above me, and pierced and broke into fragments the dark cloud which enveloped America. At the same moment the angel upon whose head still shone the word "Union," and who bore our national flag in one hand and a sword in the other, descended from the heavens attended by legions of white spirits. These immediately joined the inhabitants of America, who I perceived were well-nigh overcome, but who immediately taking courage again, closed up their broken ranks and renewed the battle. Again, amid the fearful noise of the conflict, I heard the mysterious voice saying, "Son of the Republic, look and learn." As the voice ceased, the shadowy angel for the last time dipped water from the ocean and sprinkled it upon America. Instantly the dark cloud rolled back, together with the armies it had brought, leaving the inhabitants of the land victorious.

FINAL PEACE

" 'Then once more I beheld the villages, towns and cities springing up where I had seen them before, while the bright angel, planting the azure standard he had brought in the midst of them, cried with a loud voice: "While the stars remain, and the heavens send down dew upon the earth, so long shall the Union last." And taking from his brow the crown on which blazoned the word "Union," he placed it upon the Standard while the people, kneeling down, said, "Amen."

" 'The scene instantly began to fade and dissolve, and I at last saw nothing but the rising, curling vapor I at first beheld. This also disappearing I found myself once more gazing upon the mysterious visitor, who, in the same voice I had heard before, said, "Son of the Republic, what you have seen is thus interpreted: Three great perils will come upon the Republic. The most fearful is the third passing which the whole world united shall not prevail against her. Let every child of the Republic learn to live for his God, his land and Union." With these words the vision vanished, and I started from my seat and felt that I had seen a vision wherein had been shown to me the birth, progress, and destiny of the United States.' "

A WORD OF WARNING

Anthony Sherman climaxed his recollection of Washington's words by saying, "Such, my friends, were the words I heard from Washington's own lips, and America will do well to profit by them."

Thomas Jefferson once said of our first President: "His integrity was the most pure, his justice the most flexible, I have ever known. He was, indeed, in every sense of the word, a wise, a good and a great man."

INTERPRETATION OF THE VISION

These three perils which George Washington saw all took place *on* American soil.

Peril 1: Was no doubt the revolutionary war which still continued for three years after the Lord gave Washington the vision. There was much suffering, but not as intense as the other perils which were yet to come.

Peril 2: The ill-omened spectre coming from Africa points towards slavery as the issue of a terrible civil conflict when the nation was divided and brothers fought brothers.

Peril 3: The last and most terrible of all, clearly predicts hordes of enemies from Europe, Asia and Africa, armed for mortal combat. A red light accompanies these terrible invaders - indicating they are no doubt Communists. They come by air (the cloud), land (perhaps via Canada) and sea. They devastate *all* of America, destroying cities, towns and villages. Millions are engaged in mortal conflict. Just when all seems lost, divine intervention from heaven, angels and saints descend to assist the inhabitants of America to close their ranks and win the final victory.

A special warming is given by the Angel of the Union to Americans: "LET EVERY CHILD OF THE REPUBLIC LEARN TO LIVE FOR HIS GOD, HIS LAND, AND UNION." This is an indication that in the last peril patriotism, the love of country, the respect for our constitution and our faith in God will be in great jeopardy. Already we find this to be the case. May God help us to heed the warning of the guardian Angel of America - before it's too late!

The two World Wars and the Korean and Vietnam wars were never shown to Washington. Probably because they were not fought on American soil.

73

The first war was that in which he was engaged, and the second involved a civil conflict of brothers in which the Union prevailed, and the third was concerning an invasion of European, Asian and African forces or spirits. Of the three wars, the third was by far the worst, but even so the Union prevailed.

Spiritual revival fires cleansed the land, having laid the pattern for those white stripes of purity in her continental army flag. Storms in the spiritual heavens above and bombs bursting in air became the everlasting stripes of the Union as Betsy Ross first sewed them there to a field of blue in 1777. Red stripes of courage evolved to represent a blood so precious of brave new martyrs mingled with that of Jesus a millennium before to insure a redeeming liberty for all.

American colonists eagerly enlisted to fight the yoke of an ungodly government and its curses. England, on the contrary, had great difficulty turning subjects to the battle because they had been touched by the Great Awakening also and would not enlist to fight brethren. At last King George enlisted German mercenaries into a failing effort.

Victorious in the Revolutionary War, America's continental forces mustered the moral strength to defeat the British in a second testing of the nation's right to exist in 1812.

These lines from Francis Scott Key's anthem scribbled with patriotic emotion while viewing the battle in Baltimore's bay, express the attitude of 18th century Americans:

> "Let the heaven's rescued land praise the
> Power that hath made and preserved us a
> nation. Then Conquer we must. In God
> is our trust."

Without the aid of modern communications, in less than a week the anthem was being sung throughout the colonies with swelling adulation!

But after the war, in just a few short years, individuals and states had begun to overindulge in personal liberties, no longer caring about being their brothers keepers or pleasing

God. Self-gain was becoming a wedge to divide them by the time the Continental Congress of 1787 met in Philadelphia to design a constitution of government. They guarded themselves, protecting their own interests. George Washington was summoned from Mt. Vernon to claim the committee but remained a silent member, not wishing to appear as another kingly figure of too much influence to the people of the new republic.

At last an elderly patriot, Ben Franklin - perhaps inspired by the late Whitefield - stood up and quoted Psalm 127:1, (KJV)

> "Unless the Lord build the house, they labor in vain that build it. Unless the Lord watch the city, they labor in vain that watch it."

An awesome reverence fell upon the committee who filed out of the hall in silence. Returning the next day they established prayer as the beginning of every agenda. Immediately following this decision the Constitution of the United States was formed.

Clearly God's divine hand of providence was moving again and *no where in the document do the words "separation of church and state" appear.* Where did the term come from?

The phrase was penned by Thomas Jefferson who was not present at the Congress but busy helping the French plan their revolution based on the atheistic and agnostic reasoning of existentialism. It is clear to see why God did not allow the French to win the colonies; for had they won, the nation would have never taken on a Christian character but one of total humanism.

Jefferson believed that humans and not a central government or Biblical dictates should decide the course of individuals and states other than for the causes of protection and postal services. Though an original signer of the Declaration of Independence his broad interpretation of

75

liberty allowed for a dose of [healthy rebellion to keep the powers of federal government in check], thereby planting the seed of division seceding states later used to form the Confederacy - civil war being the result.

In 1986 the Holy Spirit showed me a vision of the United States of America in the form of a patchwork quilt consisting of fifty states. Each patch seemed to be sucking and heaving at the seams as if to rip apart. The force seething beneath the blanket was that same spirit of division of Civil War days, which had not been slain but only laid dormant. Now it seems to be regaining strength, threatening to divide our nation into many factions, Christians vs. Christians and Christians vs. Humanists, Homosexuals and Abortionists. And there are new uprisings of native Indian issues and racial conflicts. Even at the time of this writing matters of Constitutional jurisdiction on abortions and flag-burnings have been turned over to state legislatures, dividing state from state as they formulate their stand, opening the door for riots and bloodshed. But in the midst of this confusion I heard the "Battle Hymn of the Republic" being sung and saw that it was the time for God's army to win souls by rushing boldly upon the battlefields! God is bringing a countermove to all of this. When Satan cries "hatred and division," the Spirit of God cries "love and unity".

Christ birthed the Church in blood. Satan had his cohorts there and waiting among the lives in Herod's courts to say that the disciples stole the body of Christ and that He had not risen. Again and again Satan moves to obliterate the liberating plan of God. Waiting in the wings were men like the Pinzons, Samuel Hutchinson, William Rogers, Benedict Arnold, and Thomas Jefferson - whose ideas of democracy were more near to anarchy than those of the Union established by the federalists.

To determine the controversial issue of whether or not the Continental Congress intended for Biblical guidance to remain a part of the government, one must observe the Constitution in the light of period writings by the same men. Clearly, they did not want to endure the tyrannies of a state church ever again but were in no way trying to exclude the guidance of the Holy Ghost from their governmental decision making processes!

"From The Bill of Rights, Article 1. Religious Establishment Prohibited, Freedom of Speech, of the Press, and Right to Petition.
"Congress shall make no law respecting an establishment of religion, or prohibiting the free exercise thereof..."

Fireworks celebrations marked the nation's unique victories on the 4th of July during the 19th century while another sort of explosion began to brew in Congress. But burning embers from both kinds spread across the continent and landed in the very places that other revivals occurred, such as St. Louis, Missouri and Azuza Street, California. In the painting one ember even illuminates the head of a Cherokee Indian chief, John Ross.

In 1838, he led his people on "The trail of tears," a forced march, one of the most ungodly atrocities of our government's abuse of the natives since Columbus's day. Before entering Newton County, Arkansas, the chief was greeted by a friendly Christian leader, Frank Villines, who had persuaded local settlers to treat the weary travelers well. In sharp contrast to former receptions of prejudiced whites, a feast and bounty of supplies awaited the Indians.

In grateful response Chief John Ross, a Christian convert through British missionaries, spent the entire night on a ridge praying for them. And before his departure he generously awarded them a large Jasper stone ring, stating, "Jasper is a hard and strong stone, lighted from inside by love. It is like the men of this ridge. Call the place Jasper." Jasper is a Biblical semi-precious stone in the new city gates of Jerusalem. Though Satan would further hinder the character of a Christian nation from forming, God continued to open windows and gates!

Wagon trains headed westward; steel mills industrialized the East; and cotton plantations rambled across the South using thousands of slaves.

Though the authors of the Constitution had stated that all men were created equal, slaves and Indians did not seem to be included in the mind of Americans at all. Reports of slaves being brutally beaten, for no other crime that attempting to worship Jesus, point towards the total hypocrisy of the Church. After working a back-breaking day in the fields, the slaves are noted to have retreated to the swamps to worship the God of the white man of Whom they had learned. At one point more than 3,000 of them were rounded up and murdered in cold blood for this so-called crime. Masters proclaiming that slaves were lesser beings, animals, found it difficult to justify their being able to think and cry out for a savior. While Americans were once again growing increasingly more selfish and hardened against the evangelical purpose of the nation, these martyrs - like modern day Russian Christians and Jews - laid down their lives for liberty with many prayers and fasts.

As I was painting the figure of one little "Mammie," I could hear in my spirit the cry of her prayers for freedom on the behalf of all who were bound physically - and especially spiritually. Prayers like hers must have rung in the ears of God so loud that He answered with the second **Great Awakening!**

Charles Finney was a forerunner of the move in the early 1850's, proclaiming that revival was as sure as seed-time and harvest. Revival would come providing all the conditions were supplied by willing men who would take hold of the horns of the altar and stir themselves to pray.

In 1858 while a simple and humble merchant, Abraham Lincoln, prepared himself for the United States Senate in the face of complex political divisions, God again began to bring forth one of the greatest revivals of all time.

In New York City the fires of the Holy Ghost began to consume an unknown man named Jeremiah Lamphier. Printing and distributing handbills to local businessmen, he succeeded in starting a noonday prayer meeting that grew to astounding numbers. Simple prayers and petitions flooded in being rewarded with continuous answers.

Newspapers began to report the happenings, and the sparks soon ignited the hearts of businessmen in all major cities until a blazing bonfire of the Holy Ghost had consumed the entire nation. So complete were the results in such towns as Louisville, Kentucky that the papers announced the arrival of the Millennium! This revival even crossed to Europe once again and touched the heart of Charles Spurgeon in England. Unlike the revival before, it did not sport the names of men as its instigators nor report sensational miracles but rather it evolved in many common people simultaneously.

Perhaps the lack of more confident leadership caused the flames to burn dim too quickly, for even though God had sovereignly awakened America to His desire for their hearts, there was not a thorough enough repentance to mend the political striving to turn hearts to feel mercy for the slaves.

Thus in 1861 the flames of the Civil War burned off the harvest fields of souls rather than the purifying fires of the Holy Ghost. America had become too lax, stiffened and resistant to her calling. The matter of greed and slavery would have to be eradicated from her spirit in some other way that she might eventually begin to share Christ's liberty with all men.

Through civil strife Satan pitted Christian against Christian, but he could not destroy the prevailing power of their forefathers' covenant with God. Though the Union flag plunged to the dust in bloody travail, its purpose as stated in the Pledge of Allegiance could not be defeated:

> I pledge allegiance to the flag of the United States of America and to the Republic for which it stands, *one nation under God, indivisible,* with liberty and justice for all.

During the throes of the battle, Bible societies from the preceding revival continued to distribute Bibles in army camps on both sides of the North/South conflict. Proportionately, they were able to distribute more of the written Word of God to the total populace than in any other period of history.

At last in 1864 Confederate forces under General Robert E. Lee, a Christian, surrendered to General Ulysses S. Grant at Appomattox. The Union would survive! Yet even as Americans rejoiced, Satan retaliated with the assassination of President Lincoln in Washington, DC at the Ford Theater. The assassin was an insane demon-possessed man whom the South neither claimed nor supported. Lincoln's death was their greatest loss of the war because his generous reconstruction plan died with him. But like a Moses he led us to the position where God had intended from the start, a fully free nation.

THE GETTYSBURG ADDRESS
November 19, 1863

Four score and seven years ago our fathers brought forth on this continent, a new nation, conceived in Liberty, and dedicated to the proposition that all men are created equal.

Now we are engaged in a great civil war, testing whether that nation or any nation so conceived and so dedicated, can long endure. We are met on a great battle-field of that war. We have come to dedicate a portion of that field, as a final resting place for those who here gave their lives that that nation might live. It is altogether fitting and proper that we should do this.

But, in a larger sense, we can not dedicate - we can not consecrate - we can not hallow - this ground. The brave men, living and dead, who struggled here, have consecrated it, far above our poor power to add or detract. The world will little note, nor long remember what we say here, but it can never forget what they did here. It is for us the living, rather, to be dedicated here to the unfinished work which they who fought here thus far so nobly advanced. It is rather for us to be here dedicated to the great task remaining before us - that from these honored dead we take increased devotion to that cause for which they gave the last full measure of devotion - that we here highly resolve that these dead shall not have died in vain - that this nation, under God, shall have a new birth of freedom - and that government of the people, by the people, for the people, shall not perish from the earth.

Lincoln also warned in a speech that men should not fail again to raise their children in the fear and admonition of the Lord, or they would not survive another battle on the continent!

America erected to the martyred president a memorial exalting his virtues as the savior of the Union and the emancipator of freedom. At last Americans were spiritually and physically ready to evangelize the world. What would we do with a liberty so great? Many diverse things.

We became the protectors and defenders of liberty worldwide. Financing missionary councils we sent out more Christian missionaries than any other nation on earth. We opened our harbors to receive thousands of emigrants eager to follow our example and embrace our liberties and the Gospel.

But we also continued to torture our slaves, abuse our Indians, embrace humanism, use capitalistic economics, legalize abortions and sexual perversions of every kind, ban God from our schools and public institutions, and allow the erection of temples to pagan gods on our hallowed land.

The result was that we fell prey to our enemies by Satan's desire to test us further. With much human sacrifice we allowed our flag to suffer more frequent travail as we car-

81

ried it across battlefield after field, of the Spanish American War, the World Wars I and II, and the Korean and Vietnam wars. When shall we ever learn that only the blood of Jesus coursing through humble hearts can heal the nations?

Americans' greatest revival is still needed to complete the vision. Oh that the consuming fires of the Holy Ghost would take hold of us before the consumption of war again.

But I believe that we are yet to come into our greatest hour of power when a revival of all revivals shall affect us from sea to shining sea!

7

THE BLOOD THE KEY

For in showing me the painting, God was giving me hope to share with you, America! Yes, there is a healing salve for your wounds, the precious blood of Jesus! Preach it! Receive it! Pray through it!

Though all the vision from Christ's wounded side to the midwest portion of the painting is bloody and tumultuous, it ends in the serene and strong portrait of an eagle soaring above the American flag with its beady eyes intensely focused above the storm towards the return of the rapturing Christ and His triumphant armies.

Behold He comes with His rewards in His hands. And just as He would seem to gather the Jews through His arm stretched across the holocaust of Europe, He shall gather in those who are watching and waiting for Him among the Church.

In the fourth panel of the painting, "The Travail of the Flag", I painted the right arm of Jesus. In death it is laid down for humanity with the mark of a covenant slashed in His wrist. Eastern men cut their blood covenants in the right

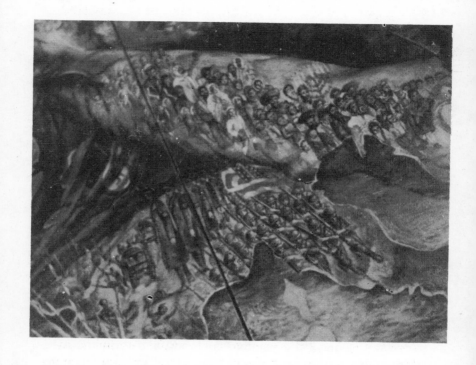

Emerging from the dark cavern of Christ's wounds, His brethren, the Jews, return to their home land in victory.

wrist. Emerging from the dark cavern of the wound is the nation of the Jews, first in their skeletal form of death from Hitler's concentration camps and then in the tattered robes of refugees. Finally a priest appears blowing the shofar (ram's horn), and multitudes are led into their homeland of Israel.

Pictured in the heart of Christ is the center of that country, Jerusalem. And highlighted there is the Temple Mount where Abraham, Father of the Jews, began to sacrifice his son. God allowed him to substitute a ram for the covenant they were cutting, and Abraham found the animal caught by its horn in a thicket. The blowing of the ram's horn represents the coming of the Messiah and the day when God will complete His part of the covenant. He did complete it almost 2,000 years later on that very mountain ridge, Morriah, in a place of execution named Gulgatha. But Israel rejected the sacrifice and entered almost 2,000 more years of dispersion.

Every year at Passover Feast the Children of Israel would tell their children, "Next year we shall eat the feast in Jerusalem." By 1940, that must have seemed like a vain legend, but in 1948 it came to pass as Israel miraculously became a nation once again! Jesus promised to return for His followers, and for almost 2,000 years we have told our children that we shall be raptured to meet Him in the twinkling of an eye (an atomic second), and today many see the promise as a fairytale. But as in the painting, Jesus, in stretching out His arm to His Jewish brothers, extends His hand to the Christian nations as well. One day they shall both look upon Him whom they pierced and recognize the raven black locks of His head as those of the Bridegroom in King Solomon's Song.

While gazing at the painting I realized that the fortified walls of the Iron Curtain had been painted against the bracing of Christ's outstretched arm. It represented how for a season, God had allowed their existence, but should He sovereignly move that arm and gather His people to His bosom, the prison walls and nations would crumble and be no more!

———

Pictured in the heart of Christ is the center of that country, Jerusalem.

God is a covenant-keeping God even to ten thousands of generations. Shall we keep His covenants in this generation or fall to His judgments? Let us be like Queen Esther and reclaim our God-given liberties of worship.

> "How can I endure to see the evil that shall come unto my people or how can I endure to see the destruction of my kindred?"
>
> Esther 8:6

Esther was willing to fast and pray for her nation that judgment against them might be removed. And God gave her favor with her king, extending the golden scepter to her for the granting of her desire. While painting the flagpole in the painting, I was seeing it tightly bound with tangled ropes. It burned with a refiner's fire until even the paints took on the appearance of fine gold. I did not tether it to the flag because I did not see it that way. Thus it seemed to serve no purpose but to be an object of beauty. Then the Holy Spirit let me see that it was shaped like Esther's scepter. Raised to the heavens it represented the favor of God granted to those whose prayers and blood had won it.

> "Blessed is the nation whose God is the Lord! and the people whom He hath chosen for His inheritance!"
>
> Psalm 33:12

Then I heard their prayers and saw that their voices caused the flagpole to be freed of its ropes. One great tassel swinging free was like the door of a huge grainery opening to loose its harvest! A fire swished from its tail and ignited the grain! And amid the grain appeared the faces of well known leaders in the Body of Christ, past and present.

At the forefront of the blaze was evangelist Jimmy Swaggart. Little did I know of the publicity smear that lay ahead for him in a few short months. Amid the crowd was

Amid the grain appeared the faces of well known leaders and ordinary people.

the face of Colonel Oliver North and many ordinary people carrying the flag and Bibles.

After the unveiling ceremony it became apparent that the fire which burned the field of faces was that which calls us to holiness. God first began to deal with the leaders and will yet consume all of the rest of mankind. The glory brings both blessings and judgments. But any good farmer knows that by burning off a harvest field, the ground is prepared for a bumper crop of the future!

I hear God calling us in America to raise our voices in prayer and to fast so that the harvest of souls might come in! And God will extend the scepter of our rulers to us so that wickedness may be quenched and a place for revival be made.

> "Shall everyone that is godly pray unto thee in a time when thou mayest be found; surely in the floods of great waters they shall not come nigh thee."
>
> Psalm 32:6

How then shall we pray? Through the blood of Jesus, the salve that heals our wounds and gives us strength in our declarations of faith! In the vision I painted one can see that the wound in Jesus' side is cut in the shape of the Sea of Galilee, the Jordan River, and the Dead Sea. His left fist glows with resurrection power and the wound in that wrist oozes with liquid light which congeals into droplets of blood that run down His arm pit into the wound. Life from heaven pours out upon the earth through Jesus' side. And just as the life line of Israel is the snow of Mount Hermon melting and flowing into the Sea of Galilee flowing into the Jordan River which empties into the Dead Sea, so is the blood of Jesus the life line of the Body of Christ, The Church!

With out Israel's full supply of water her crops fail. Likewise without a revival of the message of the redeeming blood of Jesus, we shall have a crop failure of souls and power. Some of the Church today prays to Him like a sugar-

The wound in Christ's side is in the shape of the Sea of Galilee, the Jordan River, and Dead Sea. It is the lifeline of Israel's crops as the Blood is the life of Chrisitanity.

coated Santa Claus. But Hebrews 12 :24 says there is power in the "VOICE" of the blood!

> "And to Jesus the mediator of the new covenant, and to the *blood* of sprinkling, that *speaketh* better things than that of Abel."

The blood of Abel was the blood of a martyr. He was killed on the first battlefield of recorded history. Satan had arranged his death to attack the plans of God to raise up a redeemer of Adam's race. His blood cried out to God from the earth for restitution.

> "What hast thou done? The *voice* of thy brother's *blood cries to me* from the ground!"
>
> Genesis 4:10

If one drop of righteous Abel's blood got Almighty God's attention, then how much more does the cry of every soldier's blood echo in His ears? And should not the cries of millions of aborted babies and martyrs shake the heavens? Earth is an artificial vessel, a cauldron filling up with the blood of humanity. One day on the plains of Meggido in the battles of Armageddon, Satan will overplay his hand and as the first drop of blood overruns the rim of earth's vessel, its cry for vengeance will be that which sentences him to the lake of fire forever!

In the meanwhile we have a mighty weapon to wield against him. The blood of a baby comes not from the mother nor mingles with her supply but rather from the father. Jesus' Father was the Father of lights, God Almighty, Creator of heaven and earth. His uncontaminated glory literally flowed through the veins of Jesus Christ! When His blood hit the rocks of Calvary it began to shake the heavens! There was an earthquake. The Temple veil was rent in two. It resurrected the dead patriarchs of the Old Testament, and it pleaded His cause in the belly of the earth for three days! Now it pleads and seals the covenant of God for every born-again believer who prays in Jesus' name. There is power to save in the blood of Jesus (Isaiah 53) and power to heal; even to heal a nation!

Healing shall come by result of revival in the church. To revive means to bring something back to life. New revelations are not necessary only the restoration of foundational doctrines of truth. Hidden within the attic of the Church of Jesus Christ are the treasure chests of these truths and memories of past revivals. It only remains to us in this generation to find the key and the keyhole that shall unlock them.

In the communion services of every Christian church there is a word-shaped keyhole that describes the source of liberty from sin and oppression; the broken body and blood of our Savior, Jesus Christ. Every true church of history has been birthed by the message of that redemption; the Orthodox, Catholics, Lutherans, Baptists, Presbyterians, Methodists, Episcopalians, Quakers, Pentecostals, etc. And every false church or cult has come from a doctrine of salvation by works rather than of repentance through the atoning blood of Jesus Christ.

In Song of Solomon 5:4, we see the condition of the Church, the sleeping bride:

"My beloved put in his hand by the
hole of the door, and my bowels were
moved for him."

When she hears the turning of his key in the lock, it is then that she awakens! She runs to the door but cannot find him and then to the streets where she is beaten by his adversaries. But at last she finds him and he conveys her away to the bridal chamber once and for all!

I hear and I see the key in the lock America! It is the blood of Jesus! The firey wind of the Holy Spirit from Heaven is bringing the thunder of its voice to earth again in a mighty shaking and outpouring of glory and revival! Oh for a

Like an eagle we must take courage to face our trials, searching the heavens for grace and favor.

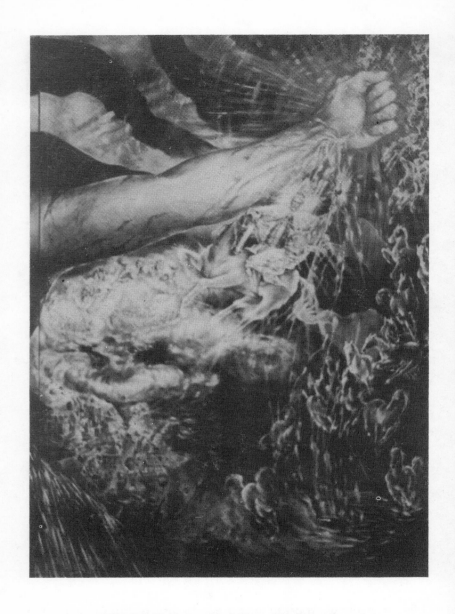

The Bridegroom is just around the corner.

thousand tongues to sing the old redemption story! When the voice of the blood in Hebrews 12:24 spoke on the day of Pentecost in the streets of Jerusalem through the apostles of old, three thousand were born into the ranks of Heaven that day!

The keyhole in the Church is the redemption story of salvation through repentance and faith in the blood of Christ. And the key is the Holy Ghost power of His voice. As the bride is stirring and waking up, we are seeing the beatings, the thirstings and the crying in the streets again. But it is a spine chilling sign to us to get ready and pray all the more, for the harvest is coming in and the Bridegroom is just around the corner to secure us in His bosum forever!

One day our flag will know no more travail, for in that day if we have carried it well, we shall lay it triumphantly at the feet of Christ Jesus and be raptured with Him to a new heaven and a new earth when our task here under this flag has been done! Amen.

BIBLIOGRAPHY

America You Are Too Young To Die
By Colonel Eugene Bird.
A tape cassette
End Time Handmaidens Inc.
Engetal, P.O. Box 447, Jasper AR 72641
c 1987.

Abbecka History Text book on American History
Pensicola Florida

From Sea To Shining Sea
By Peter Marshall / David Manuell
Fleming H. Revell Co.
Old Tappan, NJ
c 1986

Pictorial History of the United States
By James D. McCabe
J.R.Jones
c 1891

The Light and The Glory
By Peter Marshall

The Making of A Holiday
By Ann Ruff
LifeStyle Magazine
Continental Airlines / November 1987